THE BATTLE OF THE ALAMO

THE FIGHT FOR TEXAS TERRITORY

BY CARMEN BREDESON

971745

Spotlight on American History
The Millbrook Press • Brookfield, Connecticut

Library of Congress Cataloging-in-Publication Data
Bredeson, Carmen.
The battle of the Alamo / by Carmen Bredeson.
    p.   cm. — (Spotlight on American history)
Includes bibliographical references and index.
Summary: An examination of the 1836 battle, including events which
led up to it, the people involved, and the aftermath.
ISBN 0-7613-0019-8 (lib. bdg.)
1. Alamo (San Antonio, Tex.)—Siege, 1836—Juvenile literature.
[1. Alamo (San Antonio, Tex.)—Siege, 1836. I. Title. II. Series.
F390.B835 1997 976.4'03—dc20 95-49283 CIP AC

Cover photograph courtesy of State Preservation Board (Austin, Texas)

Photographs courtesy of The Daughters of the Republic of Texas Library: pp. 8, 20,
34; New York Public Library Picture Collection: p. 14; Bettmann: pp. 16, 43, 47;
Institute of Texan Cultures, San Antonio, Texas: pp. 22, 31, 35, 54; Presidial Press,
Austin, Texas: p. 24 (print courtesy Institute of Texan Cultures); The Alamo, Long
Barracks Museum, San Antonio, Texas: p. 27 (print courtesy Institute of Texan
Cultures); Archives Division-Texas State Library: p. 28; Friends of the Governor's
Mansion, Austin, Texas: p. 38; Hendrick-Long Publishing Co.: p. 40 (print courtesy
Institute of Texan Cultures); State Preservation Board (Austin, Texas): p. 49.
Map by Joe LeMonnier.

Published by The Millbrook Press, Inc.
2 Old New Milford Road, Brookfield, Connecticut 06804

Contents

In memory of my mother,
Betty Trader Thibodeau

The
BATTLE
OF THE ALAMO

Originally built as a church and school in the eighteenth century, the old Mission San Antonio de Valero, which had become known as the Alamo, fell to Mexican troops under General López de Santa Anna on March 6, 1836. The Alamo became a symbol of Texas's struggle for independence from Mexico.

1 March 6, 1836

In the still darkness before dawn, Mexican soldiers began to take their positions. They shivered in the cold morning air while waiting quietly for the battle to begin. At 5:30 A.M., General Antonio López de Santa Anna gave the order to advance, and four columns of men began their silent march to the old mission known as the Alamo. The moon cast a faint light across the desolate plain in San Antonio de Bexar, as the 1,800 soldiers got closer and closer to their target.

Inside the old adobe walls of the Alamo, exhausted Texans slept at their posts, still clutching their weapons. They were unaware of the approach of the enemy. A twelve-day barrage of cannon fire from the Mexican troops had deprived the 189 Texans of sleep for many nights. When the shelling finally stopped the night before, the Alamo defenders gratefully sank to the ground and quickly fell asleep.

During the silent advance, one of the excited Mexican soldiers suddenly shouted "Viva Santa Anna!" and "Viva Mexico!" Others took up the cry and their voices were heard by Alamo sentries, who immediately jumped to their feet and yelled to their comrades to man the guns. The twenty-one Alamo cannons were already filled with pieces of scrap metal, old horseshoes, and links of chain. As Texans began firing on the enemy, deadly shrapnel cut through the columns of advancing Mexican soldiers and killed and injured many. Their screams and cries for help filled the air around the once quiet old mission.

Wave after wave of Mexicans continued to advance until they reached the 10-foot-high (3-meter) stone walls that surrounded the Alamo. Brandishing swords and muskets, they raised ladders and began to climb. Inside the fortress, Davy Crockett and his Tennessee volunteers grabbed their long rifles and began to fire down on the enemy. There were no gun ports in the thick stone walls, so the defenders' bodies were exposed as they rose to aim their weapons. One of the first Texans to fall was William Barret Travis, the twenty-six-year-old commander of the Alamo forces. He took a single bullet to the head and rolled, mortally wounded, down a dirt embankment.

In spite of the deluge of bullets that whizzed around their ears, several Mexican soldiers managed to climb over the north wall. Once inside the compound, they ran to a nearby gate and threw it open to admit a flood of their fellow soldiers. The Texans were forced to abandon the north wall, but they continued to fire at the approaching Mexicans. Soon the south wall had also been breached.

With the enemy inside, Texan defenders began to engage Mexican soldiers in hand-to-hand combat. Bayonets flashed as they were raised to strike. Bullets whizzed through the air and struck friend and enemy alike. As hundreds of Mexican troops advanced, most of the Texans retreated into the long barracks building and bolted the doors.

Locked outside, the Mexican soldiers turned the Alamo cannons they had just captured on the reinforced doors and blasted them off of their hinges. Firing their pistols, they entered the building amid a barrage of gunfire from within. The door to the room where the ailing Jim Bowie lay on his cot was smashed open, and a hail of bullets pierced the sick man's body. A thick haze of smoke filled the dark rooms and the anguished screams of wounded men pierced the air. In just a few short minutes, Mexican and Texan bodies littered the ground, while rivers of blood snaked across the floors.

In a room near the front of the chapel, a group of terrified women and children huddled together as the fierce battle raged. A few Texan soldiers, including Davy Crockett, were also in the roofless old church when the Mexicans poured through the doors. Unable to load his rifle quickly enough, Crockett raised "Old Betsy" over his head and began to swing it as a club. He bravely fought on with six of his men until they were the only Texans left alive. A Mexican officer on the scene called a cease-fire, and the seven survivors were taken prisoner.

When Santa Anna entered the Alamo chapel to survey the carnage, Crockett and his men were brought before the Mexican general. Instead of taking the Texans as his prisoners, Santa Anna ordered their executions. Several Mexican officers objected to killing the men in cold blood, but others jumped to carry out the general's order. They drew their swords and hacked to death the last Alamo defenders.

All 189 of the Texan defenders died that day in 1836. Santa Anna gave orders to gather wood so that the Texans' bodies could be burned. At 5 P.M. a torch was put to the huge funeral pyre that had been built in the courtyard north of the chapel. Thick smoke and the smell of burning flesh filled the air in the little town of San Antonio de Bexar.

More than six hundred Mexican soldiers also died during the brief battle. Some of them were buried in nearby fields, while the bodies of others were thrown into the river. Buzzards circled in the sky around the battle site for many days. Because of inadequate medical care, dozens of wounded Mexican soldiers died in the weeks following the confrontation. Numbers vary, but Mexican casualties may have eventually totaled more than one thousand.

Fifteen women and children survived the battle, along with one male slave. After they were questioned and released by General Santa Anna, the sorrowful widows left the Alamo with their sobbing children. So many soldiers had died, both Mexican and Texan. What events had led to the disastrous confrontation between the two armies?

2 Mexico's Past

The areas known today as Texas and Mexico were ruled by Spain for more than three hundred years. In the early sixteenth century, Spanish explorers sailed their ships into waters that would one day be called the Gulf of Mexico. From some of the coastal natives, the Spanish sailors heard stories of great cities that contained palaces filled with gold. Spanish rulers directed their explorers to find the treasures and claim them for Spain.

In 1519, Hernando Cortés set out for Mexico with eleven ships and 650 Spanish soldiers. The expedition landed along the southeast coast of Mexico and established the first Spanish settlement of Veracruz. Local people in the area told the Spaniards about a mighty Aztec kingdom and its capital city of Tenochtitlán, which was home to 100,000 inhabitants. After hearing the tales of great riches, Hernando Cortés and his troops collected their weapons, mounted their horses, and set out to find the Aztec city and its ruler, Emperor Montezuma II.

The Aztecs had a highly developed civilization. During their two hundred years of power, they created a solar calendar and became skillful in the art of music and the practice of medicine. The

The Aztecs of Mexico had a highly developed society. Their cities were as grand as any in the world, and the riches they contained were plentiful.

Aztecs also were fierce warriors who often sacrificed their captured enemies. They were feared and hated by many of the other tribes in the area. As Cortés and his men got closer to Tenochititlán, hundreds of native people joined them to help defeat the Aztec Empire.

The Spaniards approached Tenochtitlán in November 1519. They were allowed to enter the city because Montezuma II thought that Cortés might be the Aztec god, Quetzalcoatl, who legend said would return from the east. Because horses and cannon were unknown to the people of Mexico, Cortés and his men did appear to be godlike as they rode into town on the backs of huge beasts.

The Spaniards were stunned by the sights that greeted them. Tenochtitlán was a magnificent city, full of painted buildings and beautiful gardens. It had at its center an enormous pyramid that was topped by two temples. In another part of town, a huge market teemed with vendors selling various kinds of clothing, food, and pottery. One of the Spaniards, Bernal Díaz, said: ". . . the great marketplace with its surrounding arcades was so crowded with people, that one would not have been able to see and inquire about it all in two days."

After the Spaniards had been allowed to enter the city, they captured Montezuma II and held him hostage for seven months. During the months of occupation, it became apparent to the Aztecs that the Spaniards were not gods. They began to revolt to try to win back control of their empire. For nearly a week, a battle between Spanish soldiers and Aztec warriors raged in Tenochtitlán. Emperor Montezuma II was stoned to death by some of his own people when Cortés forced him to go before an angry crowd to try to stop the revolt. The greatly outnumbered Spaniards feared for their lives and began to sneak out of the city. Many Spaniards were killed, but Hernando Cortés escaped, along with several hundred men.

Hernando Cortés returned to Tenochtitlán six months later with a large army. The Spanish forces surrounded the city and cut off food and water supplies to the residents. Facing the starvation of thousands of his people, the new Aztec leader, Emperor Cuauhtémoc, eventually surrendered to the Spaniards in August 1521.

After the victory of Cortés, Spain laid claim to the vast territories of the Aztec Empire. Indian cities were placed under Spanish rule, and many of the native people lost control of their lands and were forced into slavery. Colonists from Spain arrived in Mexico and established themselves in the former Indian towns. In time, the Spanish language and customs replaced those of the Indians. For more than three hundred years, Mexico and the territories to the north remained under Spanish rule.

Hernando Cortés and his group were welcomed in the city of Tenochtitlán because its ruler, Montezuma II, believed Cortés might be the Aztec god Quetzalcoatl. Two years later, when Cortés had conquered the Aztec Empire, it became evident that Montezuma II could not have been more wrong.

During the years of Spanish exploration and conquest, the French also began to send ships to the coastal areas of Mexico and Texas. The threat of French occupation and settlement made the Spanish government nervous. Vast tracts of land in Texas were left unoccupied by Spanish subjects, as few wanted to colonize an area that was home to fierce Indian tribes. In order to encourage settlement of the remote territory, Spain established five missions near what is now San Antonio, Texas, during the early 1700s. They also built a few presidios, or forts, for the Spanish troops who were there to guard the mission communities.

The Mission San Antonio de Valero and its presidio were founded in 1718. It served as a school for some of the peaceful native people and offered instruction in areas such as reading, writing, sewing, and carpentry. The Franciscan priests who ran the mission hoped to convert the Indians to the Catholic religion and make them loyal subjects of the Spanish government.

The Mission San Antonio de Valero was operated by the Catholic Church until its native population began to decrease. After it was abandoned in 1793, the old stone buildings were used as a military barracks and storage depot. For a time, soldiers from Alamo del Parras in Coahuila, Mexico, were stationed at the site. It was during their occupation that the Mission San Antonio de Valero came to be called the Alamo.

Spain also tried another method to colonize the territory of Texas. The government offered free land to Americans and Europeans who were willing to settle in the dangerous frontier areas where fierce Apache and Comanche Indians roamed. In 1821, Moses Austin was the first American to petition the Spanish government for permission to establish a colony in Texas. Moses Austin died before the plan could be carried out, but his son, Stephen F.

Austin, continued to pursue his father's dream. However, before a colony could be established, Mexico won its independence from Spain.

For twenty years, an atmosphere of unrest had been developing in Mexico. Most of the people who lived there no longer had strong ties to Spain. They had been born in Mexico and were tired of being ruled by a country in Europe. Spain's power had weakened, and it could no longer stem the tide of revolt in Mexico. Instead of engaging in war, leaders from the two sides met peacefully in 1821 and agreed to the formation of the Republic of Mexico. After three hundred years, Spain gave up its right to govern the area.

As all of the changes took place in Mexico, Stephen F. Austin was unsure whether his proposed colony would still be welcome in Texas. Would the new government in Mexico also offer free land to those who were willing to colonize its frontiers?

3 Colonization of Texas

In 1821 the Republic of Mexico approved Austin's petition to settle part of Texas, and he was allowed to travel around the territory to find a suitable spot for his colony. He selected a location between the Brazos and Colorado rivers, a site with rich soil and good rainfall. He called his headquarters San Felipe de Austin.

Stephen F. Austin returned to the United States to advertise for people willing to move to Texas. He wrote that the area was ". . . as good in every respect as man could wish for, Land all first rate, plenty of timber, fine water—beautifully rolling . . . ." Austin had no difficulty attracting colonists who were drawn to Texas by the offer of free land. Each family that wanted to farm was eligible to receive a labor of land, or 177 acres (72 hectares), while those who planned to raise livestock were to be given a league of land, or 4,428 acres (1,792 hectares). The newcomers would pay only a small title fee and be exempt from taxation for ten years.

By the fall of 1821, Stephen F. Austin was back at San Felipe. His settlers began to arrive on horseback and in wagons that were loaded with children, household goods, and tools. Each of the new arrivals spent some time exploring the land in search of the perfect

Stephen F. Austin, the "Father of Texas," issues a land title to prospective Texas settlers in 1822. True to his nickname, Austin was instrumental both in the colonization of Texas and in the fight for its independence.

spot for a homestead. Makeshift dwellings were hastily built and crops were quickly planted.

During their first year in Texas, Austin's families had a very difficult time. A severe drought ruined a large part of the crops, and Karankawa Indians attacked and killed many of the settlers. After the Indian raids, some packed up and left. In order to protect the safety of the people who remained, Austin organized a militia that gradually drove the Karankawa out of the territory.

As the atmosphere became less threatening, the area around San Felipe de Austin began to grow and prosper. The colonists had sworn to join the Catholic Church and uphold the government of Mexico in return for their free land. The Mexican government did not interfere in the lives of the colonists to any great degree, though, because the settlement was far away from any Spanish-speaking town. The officials allowed Stephen F. Austin to establish rules and keep peace in the area.

In 1824 the Republic of Mexico decided to expand its colonization laws and allow others to enter Texas. Thousands of settlers flooded into the area to claim their labor or league of land. Small farming communities were established all over east Texas. Cotton plantations and large cattle ranches also became a familiar sight in the territory.

Problems began to arise for the colonists in 1824 when Mexico decided to combine the state of Texas with the state of Coahuila. The seat of Mexican government in Texas had been located in San Antonio de Bexar until that time. After the states were combined into Coahuila y Texas, the capital was moved to Saltillo, which is 350 miles (560 kilometers) away from San Antonio de Bexar. Coahuila was allowed to have eleven representatives in the new government, while Texas was allowed to have only two. Texans, who felt that they were not being treated fairly, began to hold public meetings to demand more representation in Saltillo.

In spite of the growing atmosphere of unrest, new settlers continued to pour into Texas. By 1830 there were about 20,000 colonists in the territory. They outnumbered the Spanish-speaking population of the state by a ratio of five to one. The large number of English-speaking residents began to concern the Mexican officials, so they passed a new law in 1830. The ruling closed the

General Antonio López de Santa Anna was elected president of Mexico in 1832. Accustomed to being surrounded by luxury, as commander of the Mexican army he stood in stark contrast to the relatively ragtag collection of Texan revolutionaries he came up against.

Texas border to further immigration from the United States. In addition, the Mexican government began to impose taxes on the colonists for the first time. Mexican troops were stationed throughout the territory of Texas to collect taxes and prevent illegal entry into the state.

In 1832, General Antonio López de Santa Anna was elected president of Mexico. The following year, Stephen F. Austin traveled to Mexico City with a petition asking that Texas again be made into a separate Mexican state. In January 1834, on his way back from meeting with Santa Anna, Austin was arrested, put into prison, and charged with treason.

For eighteen months, Austin was transferred from prison to prison without a trial. During that time he wrote in his journal:

"What a horrible punishment is solitary confinement, shut up in a dungeon with scarcely light enough to distinguish anything. If I were a criminal it would be another thing, but I am not one."

Austin was finally released in 1835, and allowed to return to Texas. During that same year, President Santa Anna threw out the Federal Constitution of 1824 and declared himself to be the absolute ruler of Mexico.

When Stephen F. Austin arrived home in September 1835, he was a changed man. His days as a peacemaker appeared to be over as he issued a call to arms for all Texas colonists. Austin said: "War is our only resource. There is no other remedy. We must defend our rights, ourselves, and our country by force of arms." Messengers on horseback were sent racing across the territory with news of the impending revolt. Papers were distributed that said:

FREEMEN OF TEXAS
TO ARMS!!! TO ARMS!!!
NOW'S THE DAY, AND NOW'S THE HOUR!

In order to try to squelch the rebellion, Santa Anna sent his brother-in-law, General Martín Perfecto de Cós, to Texas. Cós and his army arrived at Copano Bay on September 20, 1835. As the Mexican troops made their way inland, they arrested a number of Texans and confiscated their weapons. General Cós arrived in San Antonio de Bexar with 1,200 men and twenty-one pieces of artillery. They moved into the Alamo barracks and positioned their cannons in strategic locations around the fortress.

General Cós knew that the colonists at Gonzales had an old, worn-out cannon that had been loaned to them by the Mexican government for protection against Indian raids. Cós sent a detach-

A brave, risky move by the colonists at Gonzales, the old cannon's firing was the first incident in the Texan revolt against the army of Mexico.

ment of soldiers to Gonzales with orders to take the cannon from the Texans. When the Texans learned of the advance of the Mexican troops, they loaded the gun and placed it under a flag that said: "Come and take it."

As the detachment of Mexican soldiers got closer, the old cannon was fired. One Mexican was killed, and the rest retreated to San Antonio de Bexar to await further orders. Although the battle for the cannon was very small, it was the beginning of the Texan revolt against the army of Mexico. When news spread that shots had been fired at Gonzales, many Texans gathered a few supplies, mounted their horses, and set out to fight for independence.

4 Texas Revolt

Four hundred men assembled at Gonzales. Most were volunteers who had left their farms and families to join the Texan army. Under the leadership of Stephen F. Austin, they began their march to San Antonio de Bexar in October 1835, accompanied by the old cannon, which was pulled by two longhorn steers. One of the volunteers, Noah Smithwick, described the appearance of the Texans: "Buckskin breeches were the nearest approach to uniform, and there was wide diversity even there, some being new and soft and yellow, while others, from long familiarity with rain and grease and dirt, had become hard and black and shiny. . . . Here a big American horse loomed above the nimble Spanish pony . . . there a half-broke mustang pranced beside a sober, methodical mule. . . ."

The Texans camped on the outskirts of San Antonio de Bexar and remained there for two months. During that time, Stephen F. Austin was relieved of command and named a commissioner to the United States. His replacement, General Edward Burleson, was not eager to lead the four hundred Texans into battle against 1,200 Mexicans. In the camp supplies were low and there was little discipline among the volunteers. Some left to check on their families, while others simply drifted away. They were replaced by new volunteers, who arrived daily as word spread of the revolt. Most of the Texans were anxious to fight the Mexicans, and they grew impatient with the delays.

Instead of ordering his troops to advance, Burleson directed the Texans to retreat on December 3, 1835. Colonel Benjamin Milam disagreed with Burleson's order and shouted: "Who will go with old Ben Milam into San Antonio?" Eager to fight, 240 men stood up and cheered. Milam shouted: "Then fall in line!" By the time the soldiers reached the outskirts of San Antonio, the number of Texans had reached three hundred.

On the cold and wet morning of December 5, 1835, the Texans entered the town under cover of darkness. They quietly made their way up and down the streets, looking for Mexican sentries. House-to-house the Texans ran, waving their weapons and bashing the doors down with tree trunks. Bullets whizzed through the air as the enemy soldiers faced each other. Soon the streets were filled with men engaged in hand-to-hand combat.

For four days and nights, fierce fighting filled the streets. On the third day, Ben Milam was killed as he led an attack. As the Texans pounded forward, nearly two hundred Mexicans deserted and headed south. Cós and his remaining forces retreated behind the walls of the Alamo. On December 9, 1835, General Martín Perfecto de Cós raised a white flag from the Alamo and surrendered his army to the small band of Texans.

Cós agreed to leave town and withdraw his army south of the Rio Grande. The Texans took possession of the twenty-one cannons in the Alamo, along with the ammunition and supplies left behind by the Mexican army. When Santa Anna heard of the Mex-

Frustrated by General Edward Burleson's inaction, Colonel Benjamin Milam took matters into his own hands and led a group, under cover of darkness, to seize San Antonio de Bexar.

ican surrender, he was furious. He immediately began to organize an army and make plans to put an end to the Texan revolt.

While Santa Anna was busy outfitting and training an army in Mexico, a group of Texans met and organized a provisional government. Henry Smith was elected president, and Sam Houston was appointed commander in chief of the Texan forces. The 6-foot-3 (190-centimeter) former governor of Tennessee was well known for his hard drinking and adventurous life. Houston's so-

After a four-day siege at San Antonio de Bexar, General Martín Perfecto de Cós surrendered the Alamo and its supplies to the band of Texans that had been led by "old Ben Milam." When General Santa Anna learned of the surrender, he vowed to put an end to the revolt once and for all.

called army was made up almost entirely of volunteers who had few supplies and even less discipline.

As Sam Houston struggled to attract and train additional soldiers, the Mexican army prepared to march north. On January 26, 1836, General Antonio López de Santa Anna sat astride his gold-trimmed saddle with a $7,000 sword at his side, and ordered his troops to begin their advance. Pack animals carried his monogrammed china and crystal glassware. In his command, Santa Anna had four thousand men, two hundred ox-drawn carts, 1,800 mules loaded with supplies, and 33 wagons full of equipment. But despite the splendid appearance, many of his men were new recruits who had little training.

The Mexican soldiers' days were filled with long marches over rugged terrain. The soldiers were ravenous, but there was not enough food to satisfy their hunger. Much of the army's food had been stored in burlap bags instead of wooden boxes, and it was ruined in the rain. To help satisfy their hunger, the soldiers ate mesquite beans from the native trees and the red berries that they found growing along the route. In addition to a lack of food, there was a shortage of clean drinking water for the thirsty men. The inadequate food and water supply led to severe bouts of diarrhea among the troops, and many men were not able to continue the march because of illness and exhaustion.

In the middle of February, when the Mexican troops had been marching for more than two weeks, a cold front blew in. A Mexican officer, Lieutenant Colonel José de la Peña, described the conditions in a journal that he kept during the advance: "We had set out with a fierce norther and had suffered all day long, facing its cutting winds and rain, and by seven that night the rain had turned to snow." He continued: "The snowfall increased and kept falling in great abundance, so continuous that at dawn it was knee deep. . . ."

The freezing soldiers did not have heavy clothing to protect them from the cold. Since there were no tents to sleep in, the shivering men gathered around a few small campfires at night to try to keep warm. Many of the pack animals died in the extreme cold, along with some of the men. By the time the Mexican army finally reached the banks of the Rio Grande on February 17, they had covered 365 miles (587 kilometers) in just twenty-nine days. At least five hundred of the soldiers had either deserted or died during the grueling march.

While Santa Anna and his troops were making their way north, the Texan rebels continued to plan their next moves. On January 17, 1836, General Sam Houston sent Jim Bowie to San Antonio with orders to blow up the Alamo. Houston felt that the 440-yard (400-meter) perimeter of the Alamo was too difficult to defend. He wanted the one hundred men who were stationed there to remove the artillery and join other units.

When Bowie and thirty men reached San Antonio de Bexar on January 19, they discovered that there was little food or ammunition in the old mission. In spite of the dismal conditions, Bowie could not bring himself to issue orders to destroy the Alamo. Under the leadership of Colonel James Neill, the men began to shore up the walls and turn the compound into a fortress. Bowie arranged for forty-two heads of beef and one hundred bushels of corn to be delivered to the Alamo, along with ammunition for the cannons.

On February 3, 1836, William Barret Travis arrived at the Alamo with a small cavalry company and assumed joint command of the troops along with Jim Bowie. A few days later, Davy Crockett and his Tennessee volunteers rode into town with their long rifles slung over their shoulders. As the number of Alamo defenders slowly grew, word reached San Antonio de Bexar that the Mexican army was rapidly advancing.

On February 12, 1836, William Travis wrote a letter to Henry Smith, president of the provisional government of Texas. The letter said: ". . . let me assure your (Excellency), that with 200 more men I believe this place can be maintained & I hope they will be sent to us as soon as possible. Yet should we receive no reinforcements, I am determined to defend it to the last. . . ."

While the Alamo defenders waited for reinforcements, Santa Anna and his army arrived on the outskirts of town. Twelve-year-

Just twelve years old at the time of the siege at the Alamo, Enrique Esparza huddled in a room near the front of the chapel for safety with the women and other children of the garrison. He was one of fifteen survivors.

old Enrique Esparza, one of the children who would hide with his family in the Alamo, later described the approach of the Mexican army. He said: ". . . I was playing with some other children on the Plaza when Santa Anna and his soldiers came up, we ran off and told our parents, who almost immediately afterward took me and the other children of the family to the Alamo." Susannah Dickenson and her baby, Angelina, also took refuge in the old mission, along with several other women and children.

After the Mexicans occupied the town on February 23, 1836, the streets of San Antonio de Bexar became strangely silent. Gone were the sounds of laughter and guitar music. Out in the square, the Mexicans raised a blood-red flag from the bell tower of the San Fernando Cathedral, located 800 yards (730 meters) from the Alamo. The flag symbolized that no mercy would be given to the Texan rebels. In response to the flag, a thunderous roar belched from one of the Alamo cannons.

Nightfall brought sounds of the Mexican army setting up camp in the fields that surrounded the Alamo. As soon as the artillery was in place, the Mexicans began to fire their cannons at the old mission's walls. It was the beginning of an almost continuous siege that would last for twelve days and nights. Inside the fortress, the small band of Texans examined their desperate situation and prayed that help would arrive in time.

5 Alamo Seige and Battle

On the first day of the siege, Colonel William Travis took full command of the Alamo garrison. Colonel Jim Bowie, who suffered from a lung disease, was too ill to continue with his duties. During the first night, there was a break in the shelling, and the Texans were able to survey the damage they had sustained. A few cannons had been knocked off of their mounts and some animals had been killed, but no men were hit. Luck had been with the Texans, but William Travis knew that reinforcements were badly needed. Later that night, Travis sent a messenger out of the Alamo with a letter that read:

To the People of Texas & all Americans in the world—Fellow citizens & Compatriots—I am besieged, by a thousand or more of the Mexicans under Santa Anna. I have sustained a continual Bombardment & cannonade for 24 hours & have not lost a man. The enemy has demanded a surrender at discretion, otherwise, the garrison are to be put to the sword, if the fort is taken. I have answered the demand with a cannon shot, & our flag still waves proudly from the walls. I shall never surrender or retreat. *Then, I call on you in the name of Liberty, of patriotism &*

[33]

everything dear to the American character to come to our aid, with all dispatch. The enemy is receiving reinforcements daily & will no doubt increase to three or four thousand in four or five days. If this call is neglected, I am determined to sustain myself as long as possible & die like a soldier who never forgets what is due to his own honor & that of his country. VICTORY OR DEATH.

Among the Alamo defenders were only nine men who had actually been born in Mexico or Texas. The rest came from twenty different states in America; six had been born in foreign countries. Tennessee was represented by thirty-three men, the largest number from any state. In the garrison were four doctors, several lawyers, farmers, frontiersmen, and adventurers. Not one was a professional soldier, but most had some experience fighting in Indian wars.

William Barret Travis, a young lawyer from South Carolina, took command of the Alamo soon after the siege began. Despite his desperate plea for reinforcements, however, only thirty-two men from Gonzales showed up to help defend the Alamo. Travis was one of the first to fall.

Jim Bowie was one of the more well-known Alamo defenders. His brother, Rezin Bowie, had designed the popular Bowie knife as a hunting tool, but Jim made it famous as a weapon.

Forty-nine-year-old Davy Crockett was a former United States congressman from Tennessee. He was famous for his colorful stories about fighting bears and alligators in the American wilderness. Twenty-six-year-old William Barret Travis, commander of the Alamo forces, was a lawyer from South Carolina. Forty-year-old Jim Bowie was famous for his skill with a knife that had been designed by his brother, Rezin. The Bowie knife had a heavy handle and a curved blade that allowed it to be thrown accurately for a long way. There were many other defenders at the Alamo who were not as well known but were just as important.

As the Mexicans continued to blast away at the old mission, they moved their artillery closer and closer to the walls of the fortress. Because there were not enough Texans to rotate duty, the men inside had to remain at their posts at all times to defend the 440-yard (400-meter) perimeter. The Texans hoped that reinforcements would arrive from Goliad, where James Fannin had four hundred men under his command.

While they waited for Fannin, a group of thirty-two men from Gonzales managed to sneak through enemy lines on the morning of March 1. As they approached the Alamo walls, a Texan sentry saw movement and fired, striking one of the volunteers in the foot. A shout went up and the sentry realized his mistake. He quickly called for the gates to be opened, and the detachment from Gonzales slipped into the Alamo.

Once inside, the thirty-two men were warmly greeted by the small band of rebels. To honor the newcomers, Davy Crockett played his fiddle and a Scotsman named John McGregor accompanied him on the bagpipes. The morale of the Texans was lifted by the arrival of the men from Gonzales. Surely James Fannin and his four hundred soldiers could not be far behind. But just two days later Travis got the bad news that Fannin and his men would not be coming to assist the Alamo defenders. Fannin believed that the Mexican army was also planning to attack Goliad, and he had decided to keep his men there to defend the presidio.

By March 5, Santa Anna had grown tired of the standoff at San Antonio de Bexar and met with his officers to plan a final assault. Many argued that an attack was not necessary, that the Texans were not any real threat. Instead of risking the lives of Mexican soldiers, why not just wait for the rebels to run out of food and surrender? Lieutenant Colonel José de la Peña wrote that most of the officers ". . . were of the opinion that victory over a handful of men concentrated in the Alamo did not call for a great sacrifice." In spite of the advice from his officers, Santa Anna was determined to launch an attack against the rebels. The corrupt and ruthless Mexican general wanted to take the Alamo by storm to increase his own honor and glory.

Inside the Alamo, Colonel Travis seemed to sense that the time for an attack was drawing near. He gathered his men before him and asked if any of them wanted to try to escape from the fort. Only one, a Frenchman named Louis Rose, chose to leave. That evening, the Mexican shelling stopped for the first time in twelve days. Exhausted Texans sank to the ground and slept, clutching their weapons to their chests. All was quiet as the Mexican army prepared to advance against the 189 defenders in the Alamo.

When the Texans were suddenly awakened by Mexicans shouting "Viva Santa Anna!," they grabbed their guns and began to fire. Each of the Alamo defenders had already loaded several guns so that they could be fired in rapid succession. In addition, the primed and loaded cannons were quickly fired into the ranks of the advancing enemy. During those first few minutes of battle, dozens of Mexican soldiers were killed and injured.

In spite of the rapid fire of the Texans, enemy forces quickly overcame the Alamo defenses and swarmed into the fort. The terrified women and children crouched together as the fierce battle raged. Almeron Dickenson rushed to his wife Susannah's side and said: "Great God Sue, the Mexicans are inside our walls! All is lost! If they spare you, save my child."

Hundreds of Mexican soldiers quickly overcame the few Texans. Twelve-year-old Enrique Esparza said: "My father's body was lying near the cannon which he had tended. My mother with my baby sister was kneeling beside it. My brother and I were close to her." The women and children were rounded up and taken outside to be interviewed by Santa Anna. After talking to the sobbing women, the general gave each of them two silver dollars and a blanket and sent them on their way.

The small group sorrowfully left the bodies of their loved ones behind as they departed from the scene of so much suffering and death. Susannah Dickenson began walking to Gonzales, carrying her fifteen-month-old baby, Angelina.

The Texans defending the Alamo, vastly outnumbered by the Mexicans, were quickly overcome. When the battle was over, all 189 Alamo defenders were dead.

6 Texan Retreat

While the Mexican army was bombarding the Alamo, fifty-nine Texas delegates met at Washington-on-the-Brazos to draft a constitution. On March 2, 1836, four days before the fall of the Alamo, the constitution was approved and Texas independence was declared. David Burnet was named the first president of the Republic of Texas, with Lorenzo de Zavala as his vice president. General Sam Houston left the meeting and headed for Gonzales to try to determine how many men had volunteered to fight for Texas.

After Sam Houston arrived in Gonzales, Texan scouts found Susannah Dickenson walking along the road into town. They quickly took her to the general so that she could give him an eyewitness account of the fall of the Alamo. The news quickly spread to the colonists that the Alamo defenders were dead and the Mexican army was on the march across Texas.

Terrified Texans gathered their children and a few belongings and began a mass exodus that came to be called the Runaway Scrape. Roads were soon clogged with families and livestock headed out of Texas. According to a slave named Jeff Parson, "People and things were all mixed, and in confusion. The children

Learning of the bloody scene at the Alamo, and fearful that the Mexican army would take over Texas, the settlers who had flocked to the region only years before burned their homes and set out in horse-drawn wagons, fleeing Texas in what became known as the Runaway Scrape.

were crying, the women praying and the men cursing. I tell you it was a serious time."

At the presidio in Goliad, James Fannin and his four hundred men prepared to retreat from the path of the Mexican army. After many delays, the garrison finally left the fort on March 19, 1836. Their retreat was slowed by the large amount of equipment that they carried. After moving ahead only 6 miles (9.7 kilometers), Fannin ordered a halt so that the men could rest for an hour. As the men resumed their march across an open prairie, the Texans saw Mexican soldiers, under the command of General José Urrea, emerging from the trees behind them. Fannin ordered his men to load the cannons and prepare for battle.

The Texans, who were out in the open with nowhere to hide, were immediately surrounded by enemy troops. Fannin ordered his men to hold their fire until the enemy was almost upon them. Then he yelled, "Begin firing." The heavy barrage of bullets and shrapnel from the Texan ranks drove the enemy to take cover in the high grass nearby. Throughout the afternoon, the armies continued to shoot at each other. In the Texan camp, the soldiers ran out of water and had no hopes of getting more. When night fell and the shooting stopped, the Texans surveyed the damage they had sustained.

Nine Texans had been killed and fifty-one wounded. The soldiers had little food or water, and their stores of ammunition were almost exhausted. During the night, reinforcements and additional cannons arrived in the Mexican camp. Since the Texan position was hopeless, the men decided to lay down their arms and surrender if General Urrea agreed to give them honorable terms.

Colonel Fannin, who had been wounded the previous day, carried a flag of surrender as he approached the Mexican camp. At Fannin's request for honorable terms, Urrea replied: "If you gentlemen wish to surrender at discretion, the matter is ended, otherwise I shall return to my camp and renew the attack." Fannin had little choice but to accept the terms or face slaughter.

The Texans laid down their arms and were marched back to Goliad under guard. For a week they were imprisoned in small hot rooms and given little food. On March 27 the captive men were taken out of their cells and separated into four groups. Believing that they were being taken to the Gulf of Mexico where they would be released, the Texans sang as they marched out of Goliad. The four columns of men, going in four different directions, were ordered to halt on the outskirts of town. There they were gunned down by the Mexican infantry.

Nearly 350 Texans were killed in cold blood that Sunday in 1836, while about 30 escaped. Texans were enraged when they learned of the massacre at Goliad. Santa Anna and his army were portrayed as barbarians, and the rallying cry for the Texan army became "Remember the Alamo!" and "Remember Goliad!"

By the time of the murders at Goliad, Sam Houston had amassed an army of about 1,250 men who were camped on the banks of the Colorado River at Beason's Ferry. Just across the river, Santa Anna was camped with eight hundred Mexican soldiers. The angry Texans were ready to fight, but neither they nor the Mexican army could cross the raging river that was swollen from days of heavy rain.

When Sam Houston learned of Fannin's defeat at Goliad, he ordered his troops to retreat to San Felipe de Austin. Houston knew that additional Mexican troops were advancing toward the Colorado River. He did not want to engage the enemy knowing that reinforcements were on the way. But after Houston gave the order to fall back, more than two hundred Texan soldiers deserted. They were anxious to fight and were not interested in running from eight hundred Mexicans.

By April 4 the additional Mexican troops had arrived. The deluge of rain had slowed somewhat, and Santa Anna's army was finally able to cross the Colorado River and continue its advance. Hot on the trail of Sam Houston, they entered San Felipe de Austin on April 7 but missed the Texan army by a few days. Amid strong protests from the troops, Sam Houston had ordered his army to retreat north to Groce's Plantation on the Brazos River. During the 20-mile (32-kilometer) march through the rain and mud, additional soldiers deserted and morale sank lower and lower.

By the time they arrived at Groce's Plantation, the Texan army numbered only nine hundred. President David Burnet sent a message to Sam Houston that said: "Sir: the enemy are laughing you to scorn. You must fight them. You must retreat no further. The country expects you to fight. The salvation of the country depends on your doing so."

In spite of the scorn that was heaped upon Sam Houston, he kept his troops at Groce's Plantation for two weeks. During that time the wealthy landowner, Jared Groce, fed the men and turned

This painting, entitled March to the Massacre, *by Sam Houston's son Andrew Jackson Houston, shows Texan prisoners being marched out of Goliad. The massacre that ensued claimed nearly 350 lives, almost twice the number killed in the struggle at the Alamo.*

his house into a field hospital to treat the sick and wounded. The plantation's blacksmith shop repaired the army's guns and artillery while the men trained. Supplies and reinforcements also caught up with the Texans. On April 11, two cannons arrived, a gift from the people of Cincinnati, Ohio.

Sam Houston finally ordered his troops to break camp on April 12, and they began to ferry supplies across the Brazos River. The Texan army marched southeast, toward Harrisburg. Santa Anna was also headed to Harrisburg, to capture President Burnet and his rebel government. The Mexicans arrived in Harrisburg just before midnight on April 14 and found the town deserted. Just a few hours earlier, Burnet and his cabinet had fled. Santa Anna's soldiers set fire to the town when they left three days later.

Shortly after the Mexican army departed, Sam Houston's troops arrived in Harrisburg. While they were there overnight, Sam Houston wrote to a friend that ". . . we are in preparation to meet Santa Anna. It is the only chance of saving Texas." On April 19 the Texans spent the entire day moving their equipment across Buffalo Bayou. By nightfall, the exhausted men were too tired to eat and fell asleep on the wet ground at the water's edge.

At the first sign of morning light, reveille sounded to awaken the Texan soldiers. They were ordered to march for two hours before a halt was called for breakfast. While food was being prepared, word arrived that Santa Anna's troops were advancing toward Lynch's Ferry on the San Jacinto River. Sam Houston immediately issued an order for his troops to move out. With breakfast left cooking over the campfires, the hungry men fell into line and began a race to the ferry crossing. Which army would arrive first and have the advantage of selecting the best spot to meet the enemy?

7 Victory at San Jacinto

he Texans won the race. They arrived in the area of Lynch's Ferry and took possession of a dense grove of oak trees that grew along the banks of Buffalo Bayou. Hidden behind the thick foliage, the Texans took a well-deserved rest and finally were able to eat breakfast. The men enjoyed a larger than usual meal since they had captured a Mexican supply boat on Buffalo Bayou that was taking provisions to Santa Anna.

At 2 P.M. Santa Anna and eight hundred Mexican soldiers arrived and began to make camp in a field that was separated from the Texan troops by a small rise. Even though Santa Anna could not see his enemy, he knew from scouting reports that the rebels were hidden in the oak grove. Santa Anna ordered a 6-pound (2.7-kilogram) cannon readied for fire. Soon the Mexicans were blasting away at the trees, in an attempt to draw the Texans into the open.

The Texan army responded with fire from the two cannons from Ohio that they had named the Twin Sisters. After firing at each other for a time, the Mexicans pulled their cannon back to safety. The Texans, encouraged by the retreat, felt that the time was ripe for a full-scale attack. General Sam Houston did not

[45]

agree, and an argument ensued between the commander and several of his officers.

In the Mexican camp, work was under way to fortify the defenses. All night long, the soldiers piled up branches, dirt, saddles, and crates to create a barrier. Santa Anna did not know how many rebels were hidden within the safety of the trees. Throughout the hours of darkness, Mexican sentries patrolled the grounds around the camp, keeping a sharp eye out for an enemy advance. At 9 A.M., General Cós arrived with about five hundred reinforcements. Santa Anna now had more than 1,200 men, compared with only 900 Texans.

Throughout the morning of April 21, 1836, the Texan soldiers were frantic to launch an attack. Sam Houston sent a patrol out to try to determine how many men were in the enemy camp. By the time the scouts returned, it was almost noon and no plans were yet under way for an attack. With the passage of each hour, additional Mexican reinforcements might be approaching. Houston's men were ready to revolt, and several officers demanded a council of war. The meeting lasted from 12 until 2 P.M.

In the Mexican camp, the danger of an attack lessened with each passing hour. As the afternoon wore on, Santa Anna allowed his weary troops to relax. They had been up all night building the breastwork around the camp, and they welcomed the chance to sleep. Santa Anna was also tired after supervising the preparations all night, and he retired to his tent. His lack of respect for the Texan army led him to completely relax his guard. He even permitted most of the Mexican sentries to return to camp, leaving no one to watch for an enemy advance.

A little after 4 P.M., while the Mexican army slept, Sam Houston saw his chance and gave the order to attack. Mounted astride

Seeking revenge for the disasters of San Antonio de Bexar and Goliad, General Sam Houston and his troops pushed to the ferry crossing on the San Jacinto River where they hoped to gain an advantage over Santa Anna's troops.

his huge white stallion, Saracen, Houston led the troops forward. With the Twin Sisters in the middle, the Texans quietly marched in two lines toward the Mexican camp. The Texan advance was hidden from view by the small hill that stood between the two camps. At 4:30, the Texans fired the Twin Sisters and the officers shouted, "Fight for your lives."

In the Mexican camp, there was chaos after the cannons boomed. Sleepy soldiers stumbled out of their tents and groped for their weapons. As they waited for orders, the Texans ran forward shouting: "Remember the Alamo!" "Remember Goliad!" In minutes they were in the Mexican camp. With guns blazing and knives slashing, the Texans showed no mercy to their enemy.

Many Mexican soldiers threw down their weapons and jumped into nearby Peggy Lake to escape the carnage. The Texans stood on the banks of the lake and fired at the Mexicans as the floundering men yelled, "Me no Alamo—Me no Goliad." Before long, the waters of the small lake were red with the blood of slain soldiers. General Houston, his ankle slashed and bleeding, rode among his men and tried to stop the slaughter. He yelled: "Gentlemen, I applaud your bravery, but damn your manners."

Although the actual battle lasted less than twenty minutes, the killing went on for hours. The Texan officers were unable to stop the soldiers as they avenged the deaths of their countrymen who had fallen at the Alamo and at Goliad. When the killing finally stopped, nine Texans were dead and thirty-four wounded. Mexican casualty figures were much higher. More than six hundred of Santa Anna's men lost their lives in the Battle of San Jacinto, and two hundred were wounded.

Hundreds of Mexicans escaped, but nearly all of them were captured during the next few days. Among the soldiers caught hiding in the marsh was a small man dressed in a private's uniform. As he was brought into camp, some Mexican prisoners gave the man's identity away when they stood and yelled "El Presidente! El Presidente!" Indeed, the captured soldier proved to be none other than General Antonio López de Santa Anna.

Men in the Texan camp were eager to hang the Mexican general from the nearest tree, but Sam Houston said no. Instead he ordered Santa Anna to send messages to the rest of his army that he had been captured and was a prisoner of the Texans. Santa Anna was to direct General Vincente Filisola, his second-in-command, to return to San Antonio de Bexar to await further orders. When Filisola received word of the Mexican defeat at San Jacinto, he withdrew not to San Antonio de Bexar but across the Rio Grande into Mexico.

On May 14, 1836, General Santa Anna and Texas President

With Santa Anna's surrender to Sam Houston and his signing of the Treaty of Velasco in May 1836, Texas became an independent republic. Just nine years later, Texas was admitted to the Union as the twenty-eighth state.

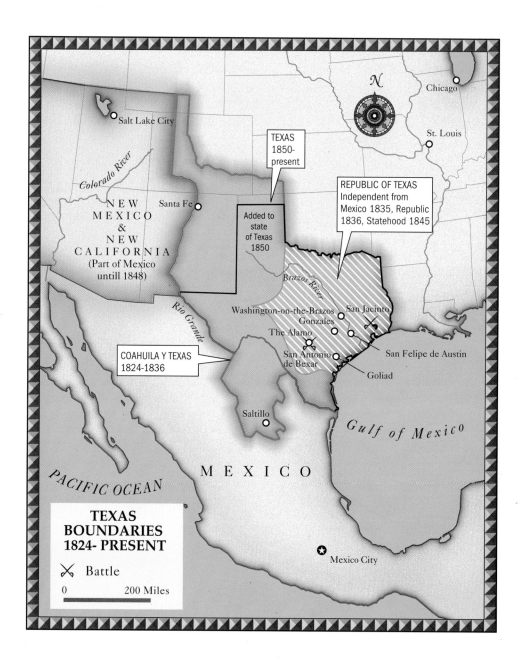

TEXAS
1850-
present

REPUBLIC OF TEXAS
Independent from
Mexico 1835, Republic
1836, Statehood 1845

Added to
state
of Texas
1850

N

Chicago

Salt Lake City

Colorado River

NEW
MEXICO
&
NEW
CALIFORNIA
(Part of Mexico
untill 1848)

Santa Fe

St. Louis

Rio Grande

Brazos River

Washington-on-the-Brazos
Gonzales
The Alamo
San Antonio
de Bexar

San Jacinto

San Felipe de Austin

Goliad

COAHUILA Y TEXAS
1824-1836

Saltillo

Gulf of Mexico

MEXICO

PACIFIC OCEAN

TEXAS
BOUNDARIES
1824- PRESENT

⚔ Battle

0   200 Miles

Mexico City

David Burnet signed the Treaty of Velasco. Mexico agreed to cease all hostilities immediately, return prisoners of war, withdraw the Mexican troops, and never take up arms again against Texas. Santa Anna was held captive for several months and then returned to Mexico. His very poor military decisions had cost the lives of hundreds of brave soldiers, both Mexican and Texan.

In July 1836, President Burnet called for the first general election to be held in the Republic of Texas. Sam Houston was elected president of Texas and Mirabeau B. Lamar vice president, along with fourteen senators and thirty-nine representatives. In addition, the Constitution was ratified and a proposition seeking annexation into the United States passed by a wide margin.

During the years that Texas was an independent republic, the population of the area increased rapidly. In 1845, Texas was finally admitted into the United States as the twenty-eighth state in the Union. Mexico never formally recognized the Republic of Texas and always had plans to return and reclaim the area. Even after Texas became a state, Mexico still felt that it owned the territory and disregarded the Treaty of Velasco. Following a border attack on U.S. troops by Mexican soldiers in April 1846, the United States declared war on Mexico. Several battles were fought before the U.S. forces captured Mexico City in 1847 and declared victory.

In 1848 the Mexican War officially ended with the signing of the Treaty of Guadalupe Hidalgo. Under the terms of the treaty, the United States gave Mexico $15 million in exchange for the lands that are now Utah, Nevada, and California, along with most of Arizona, New Mexico, and Wyoming. The conflict that arose after the bloody Battle of the Alamo eventually ended with the acquisition by the United States of nearly one million square miles (2.6 million square kilometers) of land that became the American Southwest.

Epilogue

THE ALAMO lay in ruins for ten years until the United States government leased the site from the Catholic Church in 1847 to use as a storage depot. The army put a new roof on the chapel and repaired some of the other damaged buildings.

In 1878 the army abandoned the Alamo, and a San Antonio merchant bought the long barracks of the old mission from the Catholic Church. He opened a grocery store in the building and leased the chapel for storage. The area around the Alamo grew into a bustling commercial center, full of boardinghouses, restaurants, and stores.

The state of Texas bought the Alamo chapel in 1883 and turned it over to the city of San Antonio. In 1904, Clara Driscoll, the daughter of a wealthy rancher, paid $65,000 for the long barracks and gave the deed to the state of Texas. The state named the Daughters of the Republic of Texas as custodians of the Alamo. They have maintained it ever since, at no cost to the state.

Today, the Alamo shrine consists of 4.2 acres (1.7 hectares) that are an oasis in the center of the San Antonio business district. Exhibits in the chapel honor the men who died in the battle of

1836. The Long Barracks Museum traces the history of the Alamo from the mission period through the Texas fight for independence.

THE ALAMO DEFENDERS' bodies were burned in a huge bonfire following the battle in 1836. A year later, Texas Colonel Juan Seguín found several large piles of ashes near the Alamo ruins. He collected the remains and placed them in a black-covered coffin that was buried next to the San Fernando Cathedral in San Antonio. The exact spot of the burial is not known today.

THE SAN JACINTO BATTLEGROUND is part of a 1,000-acre (400-hectare) historical park that features a monument to honor the men who won independence for Texas. Built in the 1930s, the monument stands 570 feet (174 meters) tall and houses a museum, a theater, and archives. On the battlefield site, stone markers identify the location of the Texan and Mexican camps and artillery.

GOLIAD is now the site of a memorial that was built to remember the 350 men who were massacred by Santa Anna's troops on March 27, 1836. In addition, the mission has been reconstructed and is part of Goliad State Historical Park. The presidio is under the administration of the Catholic diocese of Victoria, Texas.

STEPHEN F. AUSTIN was appointed by President Sam Houston to serve as the republic's first secretary of state. Known as the "Father of Texas," Austin served the new government for only a few months before he died of pneumonia on December 27, 1836, at the age of forty-three. At the time of Austin's death, Sam Houston issued a proclamation that read: "The Father of Texas is no more. The first pioneer of the wilderness has departed."

Around the old mission known as the Alamo grew the city of San Antonio.
The chapel can be seen at the right side of this 1890 photograph.

SAM HOUSTON served as president of the Republic of Texas from 1836 to 1838 and again from 1841 to 1844. After Texas became a state in 1845, Houston was elected a United States senator, a position he held for thirteen years. Houston was elected governor of Texas in 1859 but was deposed from that office in 1861. He had refused to swear allegiance to the Confederacy after Texas seceded from the Union during the Civil War. Sam Houston died on July 26, 1863, at the age of seventy and was survived by his wife and eight children.

SANTA ANNA was elected president of Mexico several times after his defeat at San Jacinto, but his dictatorial policies led to his overthrow. He spent several years in exile in Cuba before being allowed to return to Mexico City in 1874. He died on June 20, 1876, at the age of eighty-two.

SUSANNAH DICKENSON related the sad story of the fall of the Alamo many times. She visited the site again in 1881, forty-five years after her husband was killed fighting for Texas independence. With tears in her eyes, she pointed out important details of the battle as she remembered them. She died in 1883 at the age of sixty-eight.

ANGELINA DICKENSON was known as the "Babe of the Alamo." For many years she kept a ring that William Travis had placed on a string around her neck just before the battle. The ring is now on display in the Alamo museum. Angelina died at age thirty-seven in Galveston, Texas.

ENRIQUE ESPARZA, the twelve-year-old boy who survived the Alamo battle, became a farmer and had five children of his own. He remained in the San Antonio area and told his story many years later to a newspaper reporter. He recalled that day in the plaza when he first saw Santa Anna. "He had a hard and cruel look and his countenance was a very sinister one. It has haunted me ever since I last saw it, and I will never forget the face and figure of Santa Anna." Enrique Esparza died on December 20, 1917, at the age of eighty-nine.

THE TWIN SISTERS cannons became the property of the United States after Texas was admitted to the Union. They were taken to an arsenal in Louisiana and remained there until the state of Louisiana returned them to Texas in 1862. They were last seen in a vacant lot in Houston, along with several other old cannons. Today, their location is unknown.

TEXAS continued to grow, and by 1860 had 600,000 residents, many of whom owned slaves. With the outbreak of the Civil War, Texas seceded from the Union to become a Confederate state on March 2, 1861. Little action occurred on Texas soil; but the state contributed supplies of cotton and ammunition to the rebel army.

After the end of the Civil War in 1865, a new industry quickly grew in Texas. The state's huge expanses of rangeland were perfect feeding grounds for millions of cattle. Texas became the starting point for trail drives that moved enormous herds north to Kansas and Missouri. The thousands of cowboys who rode the herds became the subjects of legends.

By 1900, Texas had a population of more than three million residents. The year 1901 brought with it the eruption of the world's largest oil gusher at Spindletop, near Beaumont, Texas. The discovery of additional huge Texas oil fields led to the development of the state's valuable petroleum industry. Oil drilling and refining became big business, and droves of job seekers continued to push the state's population figures higher and higher. In 1994, Texas overtook New York to become the second most populous state in the Union, with 18.4 million residents.

Chronology

1521   Hernando Cortés defeats the Aztec Empire and claims Mexico for Spain

1718   The Mission San Antonio de Valero is founded

1821   Mexico wins independence from Spain

Stephen F. Austin establishes a colony at San Felipe de Austin

1824   Texas and Coahuila are combined into one Mexican state

1834   Stephen F. Austin imprisoned in Mexico City

1835   Santa Anna seizes absolute power in Mexico and throws out the Federal Constitution

October: General Cós defeated by the Texan army in the Siege of Bexar

1836   January 26: Santa Anna's army begins its march to Texas

February 23: Siege of the Alamo begins

March 2: Texas independence declared and a constitution approved at Washington-on-the-Brazos

March 6: The Alamo falls

March 27: Fannin and 350 Texans executed at Goliad

April 21: Santa Anna's troops defeated by Texans at Battle of San Jacinto

1845   Texas becomes the twenty-eighth state in the Union

1848   Mexico cedes to the United States lands that make up much of the American Southwest

Sources

The battle of the Alamo is a cornerstone of Texas history. The 189 defenders of the old fortress were heroes who inspired others to take up the call and fight for Texas. A visit to the Alamo always leaves me with feelings of awe that so few faced so many on that small field of battle. A shiver runs up my spine every time I walk through the chapel and look into the tiny room where the women and children hid on that terrible day in 1836. And I feel sadness when I enter the long barracks and stand on the same ground where so many soldiers died.

Visiting the San Jacinto battlefield is also a moving experience. There the tables were turned on Santa Anna and his troops as they became targets of the Texan army's fury. Standing on the banks of Peggy Lake, one can imagine the scene as dozens of Mexican soldiers were gunned down in the water. On the day that I visited the lake, fishermen sat in the warm afternoon sun, casting their lines into water that had once turned red with blood. No longer did screams and gunshots fill the air. They had been replaced with the sounds of birds and the gentle song of the wind.

In addition to my trips to historical sites, I read many fine books that helped to paint a picture for me of the colorful history of Texas. The following is a list of some of the valuable sources that I used in the preparation of this book:

Daughters of the Republic of Texas (compiled by). *The Alamo: Long Barracks Museum*. Dallas: Taylor Publishing Co., 1986.

Fehrenbach, T. R. *Lone Star*. New York: Collier Books, 1985.

Groneman, Bill. *Alamo Defenders*. Austin: Eakin Press, 1990.

Hardin, Stephen. *Texian Iliad*. Austin: University of Texas Press, 1994.

Lord, Walter. *A Time to Stand*. Lincoln: University of Nebraska Press, 1961.

Peña, José Enrique de la. Translated by Carmen Perry. *With Santa Anna in Texas*. College Station: Texas A&M University Press, 1975 (translation copyright).

Walraven, Bill and Marjorie. *The Magnificent Barbarians*. Austin: Eakin Press, 1993.

Further Reading

Baquedano, Elizabeth. *Aztec, Inca & Maya*. New York: Alfred A. Knopf, 1993.

Bredeson, Carmen. *The Spindletop Gusher*. Brookfield, Conn.: The Millbrook Press, 1996.

Jacobs, William. *Cortés: Conqueror of Mexico*. New York: Franklin Watts, 1994.

Ragsdale, Crystal. *Women and Children of the Alamo*. Austin: State House Press, 1994.

Stefoff, Rebecca. *Independence and Revolution in Mexico*. New York: Facts on File, 1993.

Tolliver, Ruby. *Santa Anna: Patriot or Scoundrel*. Dallas: Hendrick-Long Publishing Company, 1993.

Index